D0534821

Text copyright © 1987 by Melanie and Christopher Rice
Illustrations copyright © 1987 by Kingfisher Books Ltd.

Library of Congress Cataloging-in-Publication Data
Rice, Melanie.
    All about me.

    Summary: Introduces basic concepts about the human
body, everyday activities, and the world surrounding
children.
    1. Children—Juvenile literature.   2. Human behavior—
Juvenile literature.   [1. Human behavior.   2. Body,
Human.   3. Family life]   I. Rice, Chris.   II. Smith,
Lesley, ill.   III. Title.
HQ781.R52   1988   305.2'3   87-15498
ISBN 0-385-24281-6
ISBN 0-385-24282-4 (lib. bdg.)

First Edition in the United States of America
All Rights Reserved
Printed in Hong Kong

MELANIE and CHRIS RICE

ALL ABOUT ME

Illustrated by
Lesley Smith

Doubleday & Company, Inc.
Garden City, New York

Contents

My family   8

My home   10

Growing plants   12

My pets   14

Playing   16

Inside my body   18

Food   20

My skin and hair   22

My eyes   24

My nose, tongue, and ears   26

Babies   28

People who care for me   30

At the doctor   32
At the dentist   33

Numbers   34

Talking and writing   36

Sounds   38

Story telling   40

Let's celebrate   42
Picture Quiz   44   Index   45

My family

Everyone is part of a family.

You can be part of
a small family.

You can be part of a large family.

When people marry, they become part of
a new family. Everyone is happy, and the
two families celebrate together.

A family tree

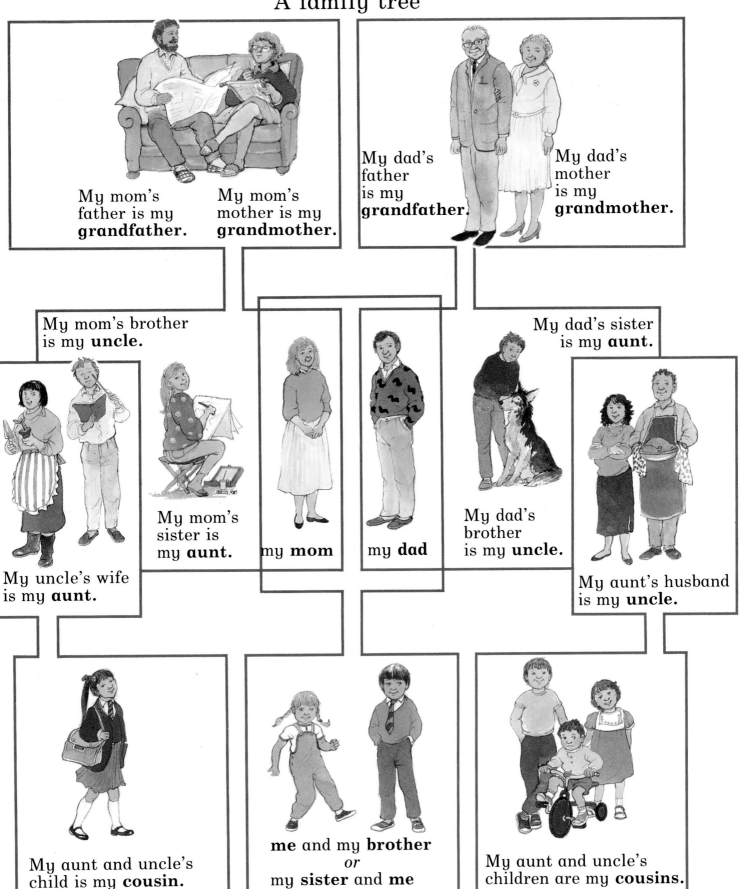

My mom's father is my **grandfather.**

My mom's mother is my **grandmother.**

My dad's father is my **grandfather.**

My dad's mother is my **grandmother.**

My mom's brother is my **uncle.**

My mom's sister is my **aunt.**

my **mom**

my **dad**

My dad's brother is my **uncle.**

My dad's sister is my **aunt.**

My uncle's wife is my **aunt.**

My aunt's husband is my **uncle.**

My aunt and uncle's child is my **cousin.**

me and my **brother**
or
my **sister** and me

My aunt and uncle's children are my **cousins.**

My home

Home is where you live.

round house

flat-roof house

tent

stilt house

bamboo house

sampan

cottage

mobile home

turf-roof cabin

yurt

apartments

Home can be a house, a tent, a boat, a caravan, or an apartment.

People's homes are different outside and inside, too.

Decorating the home

Can you find these things in the pictures?

rug

screen

cushions

vases of flowers

photograph

picture

Growing plants

It's fun to grow plants at home in a window box, in pots, or in a garden.

greenhouse

fork

spade

watering can

wheelbarrow

fork

trowel

12

Watching a seed grow

Line a glass jar with tissues or blotting paper. Place a few green bean seeds or fresh lima beans between the glass and the paper so that you can see them. Fill the jar with water and keep it in a warm place.

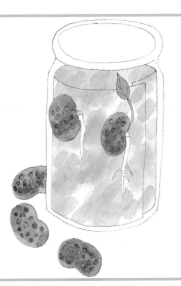

The first thing you will see is a white root growing down.

Next a shoot will begin to push upward toward the light.

At the top of the shoot, leaves will unfold.

lawn mower

rake

Looking after a garden is hard work. You need lots of tools.

Look for these in the garden.

strawberry

lettuce

aster

rose

green bean

sweetpea

hollyhock

pansy

tomato

Which ones can you eat?

My pets

Pets are animals that live with us.
Owning a pet can be fun, but remember:
animals need a lot of looking after.

Pets need fresh food, clean water . . .

. . . and plenty of exercise.

14

Most animals keep themselves and their homes
clean, but you will have to . . .

. . . change bedding . . . brush coats . . .

. . . clean the bottom of tanks and cages.

Which home would you put
these pets in?

Playing

Skipping games

Mother, mother, I feel sick,
Send for the doctor, quick,
quick, quick.
In came the doctor,
In came the nurse,
In came the lady with the
    alligator purse.

Clapping games

Pat-a-cake, pat-a-cake,
baker's man,
Bake me a cake as
fast as you can;
Pat it and prick it,
and mark it with B,
Put it in the oven for
baby and me.

Jumping and dancing games

leapfrog   **ring-a-roses**   **hopscotch**

16

Do you know these games?

baseball

soccer

cricket

volleyball

tennis

blindman's buff

tag

marbles

17

Inside my body

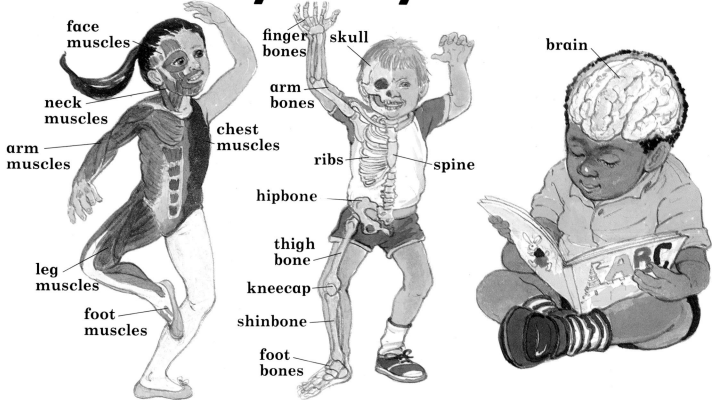

face muscles
neck muscles
arm muscles
leg muscles
foot muscles
chest muscles

finger bones
skull
arm bones
ribs
spine
hipbone
thigh bone
kneecap
shinbone
foot bones

brain

Beneath your skin are your muscles. You use your muscles to run, jump, twist, turn, and stretch.

Under your muscles are more than two hundred bones that join together to make your skeleton.

Inside your head is your brain. Your brain speeds messages to every part of your body, telling it what to do.

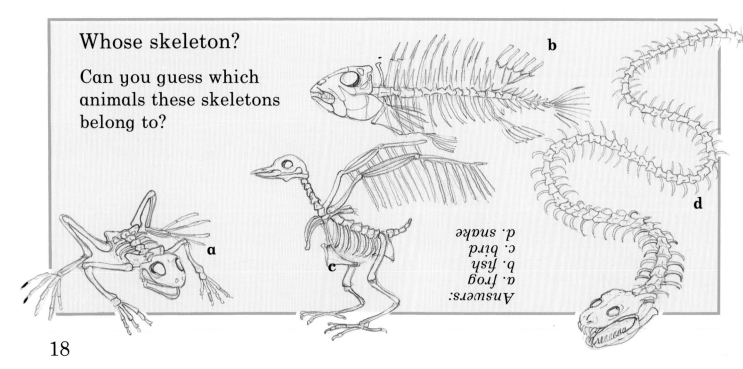

Whose skeleton?

Can you guess which animals these skeletons belong to?

a

b

c

d

Answers:
a. frog
b. fish
c. bird
d. snake

18

windpipe

lungs

heart

veins
(blue)

arteries
(red)

food
tube

stomach

small
intestine

Under your ribs, your lungs breathe in clean air and push out used air. Your blood then carries the air to every part of your body.

Your heart pumps blood around your body. Arteries carry the blood from your heart and veins carry it back again.

After you chew and swallow food, it goes to the stomach. There it is mixed with juices and turned into a liquid. The liquid passes to the small intestine, where it is squeezed even smaller. Your blood picks up useful food from the liquid. The waste food your body does not need is pushed out when you go to the toilet.

Cells

The smallest thing inside you is a cell. You have many kinds of cells in your body. Billions of them work together to make up your body. You cannot see a cell by itself because it is so small.

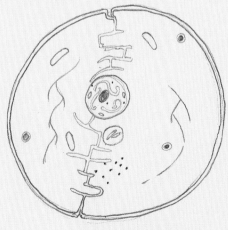

blood cell drawn much bigger

The blood carries food around the body, and so your body must turn the food you eat into bits as small as cells.

Food

Food gives you energy . . . keeps you healthy . . . makes you strong.

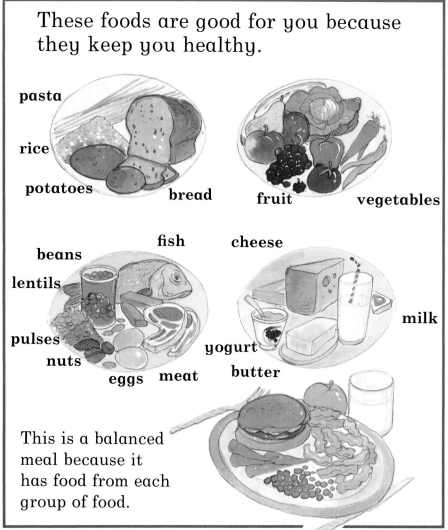

These foods are good for you because they keep you healthy.

pasta

rice

potatoes

bread

fruit

vegetables

beans

lentils

fish

cheese

pulses

nuts

eggs

meat

yogurt

butter

milk

This is a balanced meal because it has food from each group of food.

Everyone eats different kinds of food.

Italian spaghetti

roast meat and vegetables

German sausage

Food comes from animals.

Food comes from plants.

How many of these dishes have you eaten?

Indian curry and rice

Chinese noodles

Turkish kabobs

French cheese and onion quiche

Greek stuffed grape leaves

Italian pizza

American salad

Mexican tortillas

Jamaican salt-fish pie

Dutch pancakes

21

My skin and hair

No one looks the same as anyone else.

We all have chemicals called pigments in our skin and hair that make the color. Everyone has different amounts of pigments, so everyone looks different.

Touching

Your skin is covered with tiny hairs. You can see them with a magnifying glass. Nerves inside your skin at the end of each hair tell your brain when something is touching you.

See if you can touch someone's arm without their feeling you.

Goose bumps

When you are hot, you sweat. Your skin sends out little drops of water to cool you down. When you become cold, you shiver to warm yourself. Sometimes the hairs on your skin stand on end.

The upright hairs pinch your skin into goose bumps.

Fingerprints

The skin on your fingertips makes a pattern. Everyone's fingerprints are different.

Soak a piece of sponge in thick poster paint. Dab a finger onto the sponge.

Then press it firmly on a sheet of paper.

Camouflage

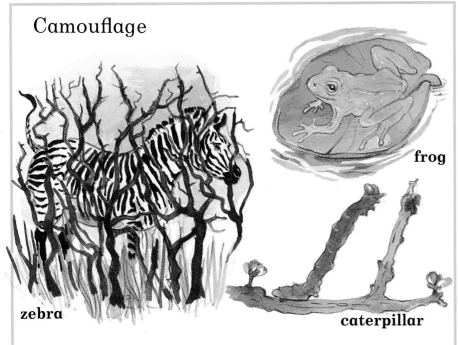

frog

zebra

caterpillar

Some animals have hair and skins that match the places where they live, and so it is hard to see them.

Did you know?

A chameleon can change the color of its skin to match the place where it is.

23

My eyes

When we look at our eyes, these are the parts we can see.

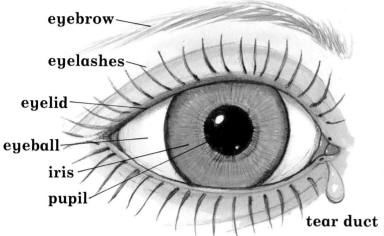

eyebrow
eyelashes
eyelid
eyeball
iris
pupil
tear duct

When you look at something, light bounces off it and enters your eyes through the pupils.

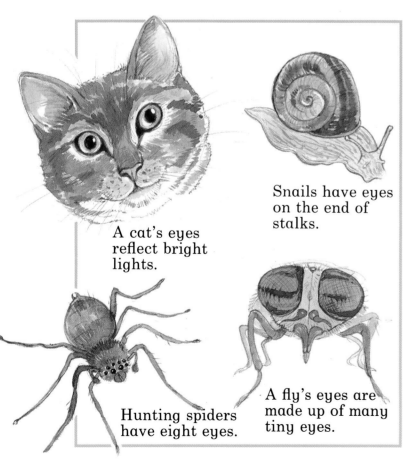

A cat's eyes reflect bright lights.

Snails have eyes on the end of stalks.

Hunting spiders have eight eyes.

A fly's eyes are made up of many tiny eyes.

Play tricks on your eyes

Look at the black squares. After a while, you will see gray blobs appear in the yellow spaces.

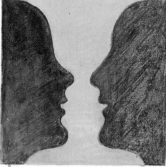

Look carefully at this picture. What do you see? (A vase or two faces?)

Press your nose slowly against the middle of this picture. What happens to the fisherman?

Can you see a number?

Eyes that see in the dark

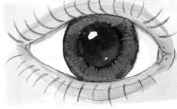

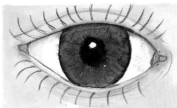

When it is dark, your pupils open to take in more light so you can see. Animals that look for food at night have big pupils to help them see.

Seeing with your hands

Blind people cannot see. Often they tell what things are by touching them.

Put some toys in a box. Choose ones that feel different. Tie a blindfold over your eyes.

Guess what each toy is by touching it.

A near-sighted person sees this.

Some people cannot see clearly. They go to an optician, who makes a pair of glasses for them. The lenses in front of their eyes help them see more clearly.

A person with good eyesight sees this.

My nose, tongue, and ears

Your nose helps you smell.

Mmmm . . . which things make your mouth water?

When your mouth waters, it is getting ready for food.

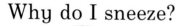

Your tongue helps you taste food. It has bumps on it called taste buds, which taste sweet, sour, salty, and bitter food.

Why do I sneeze?

You sneeze because your nose is trying to blow away something tickling inside it.

A tasting and smelling game

Put a little of different kinds of food into jars. Tie on a blindfold.

Can you guess what is in each jar, first by its smell, then by its taste?

What happens if you hold your nose while you are tasting?

You can see only part of your ear.
The rest of it is inside your head.

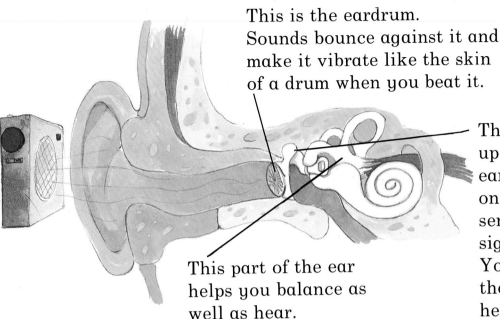

This is the eardrum.
Sounds bounce against it and
make it vibrate like the skin
of a drum when you beat it.

These three bones pick
up the vibrations of the
eardrum and pass them
on to the inner ear. It
sends the vibrations as
signals to the brain.
Your brain understands
the signals, and so you
hear.

This part of the ear
helps you balance as
well as hear.

How well can you hear?

Cup your hand around your ear.
Sounds will be louder because
you are making your ear bigger.
Deaf people cannot hear well.
Once they used ear trumpets to
make sounds louder, but today
they wear small hearing aids.

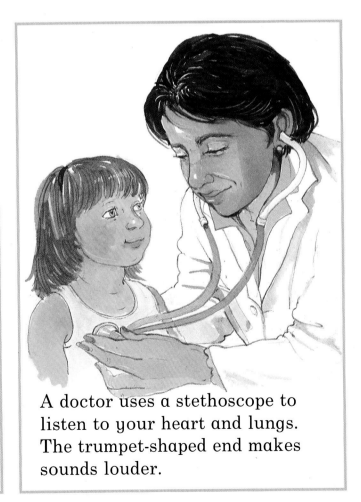

A doctor uses a stethoscope to
listen to your heart and lungs.
The trumpet-shaped end makes
sounds louder.

Babies

Everyone starts life as a baby, and this is how babies begin.

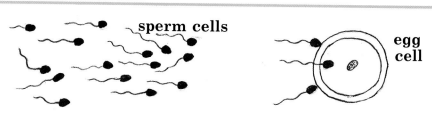

sperm cells

egg cell

A baby starts when a sperm cell from the father joins with an egg cell inside the mother.

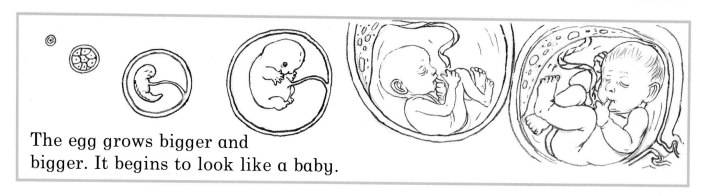

The egg grows bigger and bigger. It begins to look like a baby.

As the baby grows bigger, the mother's tummy grows bigger, too. Sometimes the baby can be felt kicking and turning around inside. After nine months, the baby is ready to be born.

The mother may go to the hospital. A midwife and a doctor help the mother give birth. Slowly her muscles push the baby out into the world.

Mom and Dad welcome the new baby.

Babies need . . .

. . . sleep . . .   . . . warmth . . .   . . . food and drink.

Babies cannot talk.
They cry when they
want something.

Everyone helps
look after them.

Babies grow and grow
and grow.

People who care for me

The world is full of people who care for us and make sure we are safe.

Can you find these in the picture?

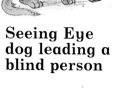

Seeing Eye dog leading a blind person

ambulance worker

fire fighter

policewoman

teachers

STOP   **LOOK**   **LISTEN**

Stop near the curb. Look all around. Make sure nothing is coming.

Then walk straight across. Keep looking and listening while you cross the road.

At the doctor

You go to the doctor when you are ill.
The doctor asks what the matter is and
then takes a good look at you.

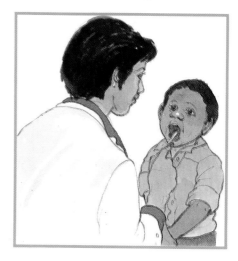

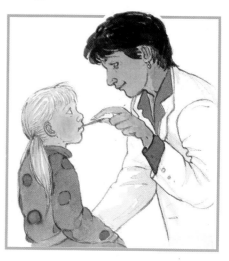

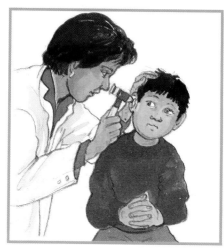

The doctor may examine your throat to see if it is sore.

The doctor may take your temperature with a thermometer to find out how hot you are.

The doctor may look in your ears with a light to see if they are clear.

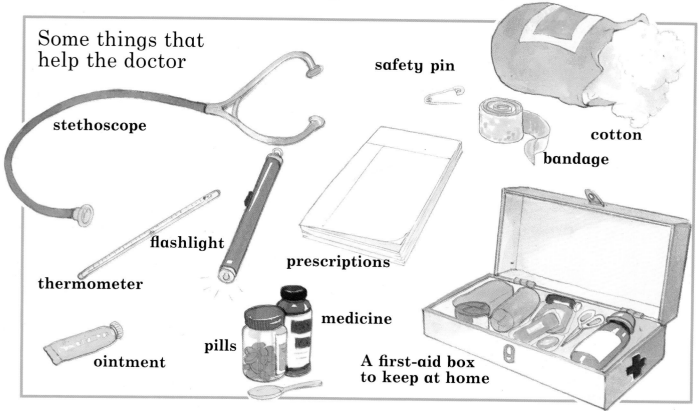

Some things that help the doctor

stethoscope

safety pin

cotton

bandage

flashlight

prescriptions

thermometer

ointment

pills

medicine

A first-aid box
to keep at home

At the dentist

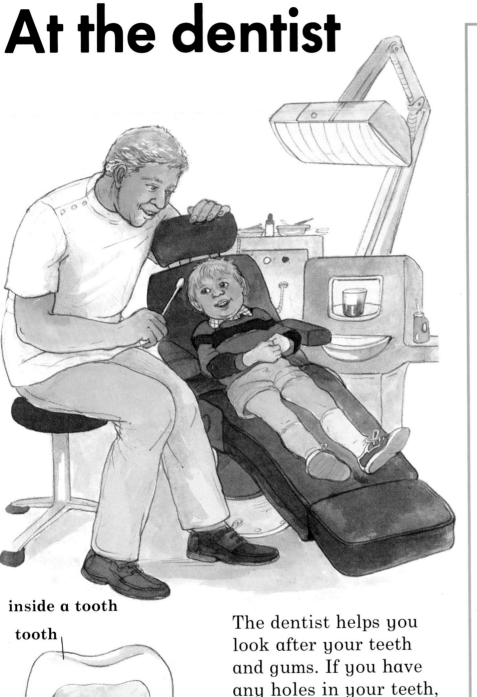

Teeth are shaped for eating food.

sharp
canines
for tearing

square flat
incisors for
cutting

square molars
for chewing

tiger

cow

beaver

inside a tooth

tooth

gum

root

nerves

The dentist helps you look after your teeth and gums. If you have any holes in your teeth, the dentist fills them with metal or plastic to stop them from getting bigger and giving you a toothache. You can look after your teeth by brushing them after meals and before you go to bed.

Can you guess which kinds of teeth these animals have?

Numbers

Numbers can be written in different ways.

	1	2	3	4	5	6	7	8	9	10
Chinese	一	二	三	四	五	六	七	八	九	十
Bengali	১	২	৩	৪	৫	৬	৭	৮	৯	১০
Hindi	१	२	३	४	५	६	७	८	९	१०
Arabic	١	٢	٣	٤	٥	٦	٧	٨	٩	١٠

Numbers people used to write long ago.

Ancient Egyptian	I	II	III	IIII	III II	III III	IIII III	IIII IIII	III III III	∩
Roman	I	II	III	IIII	V	VI	VII	VIII	IX	X

Numbers are everywhere.

34

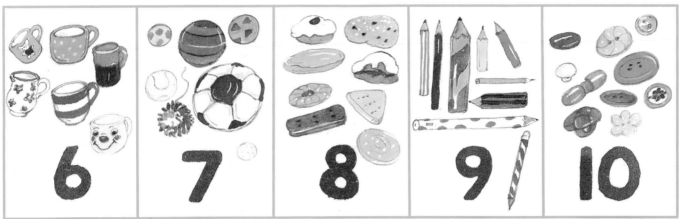

Numbers tell us how heavy we are and how tall we are. Do you know your height and weight?

measure

scales

Shopkeepers use scales to weigh food.

Sometimes we use scales to weigh food for cooking.

Packages and cans have weights marked on their labels.

Talking and writing

Babies make sounds as soon as they are born. By watching their parents, they learn to smile when they are happy.

By listening to everyone around them, they learn to say words.

People speak different languages. Some people speak more than one language.

Often we can understand people without hearing them speak. What are these people saying?

We can write down words on paper.

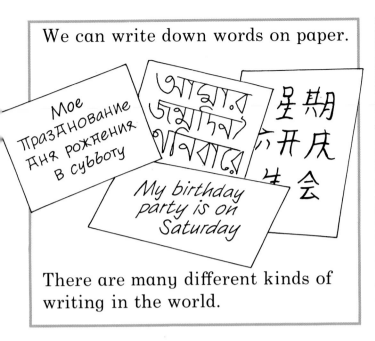

Мое
Празднование
дня рожнения
в субботу

আমার
জন্মদিন
শনিবারে।

星期
六开庆
生会

My birthday
party is on
Saturday

There are many different kinds of writing in the world.

The first books were written down by hand. It took months to make one copy.

Writing letters

You need to write the address of the person you are writing to on the envelope.

Sam Smith
5, High Street
Newtown
Colo. 33212

Then you stick on a stamp and post the letter.

A mailman collects the letters. At the post office your letter is put with others going to the same place.

Another mailman delivers the letter to the address you wrote on the envelope.

Sounds

Ssh . . . listen! The world
is full of sounds.

You can make many sounds with your voice.

whispering

shouting

singing

Making sound patterns

With your hands, try to beat out or clap the rhythm of this nursery rhyme.

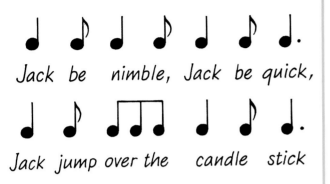

Jack be nimble, Jack be quick,

Jack jump over the candle stick

Making music

Pour different amounts of water into glass bottles. Gently tap the bottles with a spoon. Each bottle will play a different note.

Playing musical instruments in an orchestra

39

Story telling

Stories can be read . . .

. . . and danced . . .   . . . and sung . . .   . . . and acted out on a stage.

Stories can be told without using words.

Films tell stories.

40

Sometimes puppets take the place of people in stories.

Punch and Judy

shadow puppet

string puppet

hand puppet

Making a mask

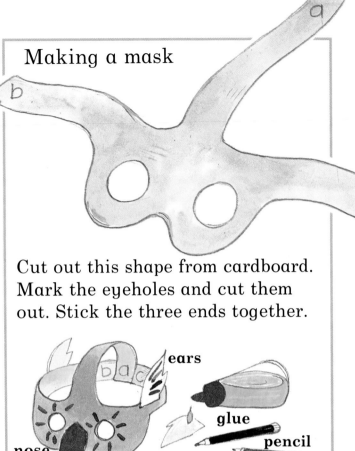

Cut out this shape from cardboard. Mark the eyeholes and cut them out. Stick the three ends together.

ears

glue

pencil

nose

Dressing-up things

41

Let's celebrate

Christmas

Chinese New Year

Caribbean Carnival

Easter

Japanese Children's Day

Muslim Eid

American Thanksgiving

Jewish Hanukkah

Hindu Dewali

42

Festivals are days made special by singing, dancing, praying, feasting, and giving presents.

Can you match these objects with the festivals?

Praying is an important part of many festivals. Here are some of the places where people pray.

shrine

synagogue

mosque

temple

church

You have your own special day or festival once a year – your birthday!

Picture quiz

Look back in the book and see if you can find these things. The numbers tell you which page they are on.

16

25

10

12

36

43

14

40

29

34

33

21

Index

To find *see page*

A
animals   14, 15, 21
arteries   19

B
babies   28, 29, 36
beaver   33
birthdays   43
blindness   25
blood   9
body   18, 19
bones   18
books   37
brain   18, 27

C
camouflage   23
Caribbean carnival   42
Carvinal   42
cat   24
caterpillar   23
cells   19
chameleon   23
Children's Day   42
Chinese New Year   42
Christmas   42
cow   24

D
deafness   27
dentist   33
Dewali   42
doctor   27, 28, 32

E
ear   27, 32
eardrum   27
Easter   42
Eid   42
eyes   24, 25

F
families   8, 9
festivals   42, 43
fingerprints   23
flowers   12, 13
fly   24
food   19, 20, 21

G
games   16, 17
gardens   12, 13
glasses   25
goose bumps   22
growing   29, 35

H
hair   22
Hanukkah   42
hearing   27
hearing aids   27
heart   19
height   35
homes   10, 11
houses   10, 11

L
languages   36
lungs   19

M
masks   41
midwife   28
muscles   18, 28
music   39
Muslim   42

N
nerves   19, 22, 33
nose   26
numbers   34, 35

O
optician   25
orchestra   39

P
pets   14, 15
pigments   22
plants   12, 13, 21
praying   43
puppets   41

S
scales   35
seeds   13
seeing   24, 25
shivering   22
skeleton   18
skin   18, 22
smelling   26
snail   24
sneezing   26
sounds   27, 36, 38, 39
spider   24
stethoscope   27, 32
stomach   19
sweating   22

T
tasting   26
teeth   33
Thanksgiving   42
tiger   33
tongue   26
touching   18

V
vegetables   12, 13, 20
veins   19

W
weight   35
window box   12
writing   7

Z
zebra 23